MACHINES THAT WON THE WAR

MACHINES AND WEAPONRY OF WORLD WAR II

Charlie Samuels

Gareth Stevens
Publishing

Please visit our website, www.garethstevens.com. For a free color catalog of all our high-quality books, call toll free 1-800-542-2595 or fax 1-877-542-2596.

Library of Congress Cataloging-in-Publication Data

Samuels, Charlie, 1961-
 Machines and weaponry of World War II / Charlie Samuels.
    p. cm. — (Machines that won the war)
 Includes index.
 ISBN 978-1-4339-8608-6 (pbk.)
 ISBN 978-1-4339-8609-3 (6-pack)
 ISBN 978-1-4339-8607-9 (library binding)
 1. World War, 1939-1945—Equipment and supplies—Juvenile literature. 2. Military weapons—History—20th century—Juvenile literature. I. Title.
 D743.7.S25 2013
 940.54—dc23
                            2012018392

Published in 2013 by
Gareth Stevens Publishing
111 East 14th Street, Suite 349
New York, NY 10003

© 2013 Brown Bear Books Ltd.

For Brown Bear Books Ltd:
Editorial Director: Lindsey Lowe
Managing Editor: Tim Cooke
Children's Publisher: Anne O'Daly
Art Director: Jeni Child
Designer: Lynne Lennon
Picture Manager: Sophie Mortimer
Picture Researcher: Andrew Webb

Picture Credits
Front Cover: Shutterstock: Stephen Meese

All photographs Robert Hunt Library except: **Mike Hoffman**: 26; **Shutterstock**: Paul Drabot 19t, 41, Sergey Kamshylin 44, Lightplayer 38, Maxim Lysenko 36, Stephen Meese 7, Phantom 20, Trinacria Photo 30l, Rob Wilson 16; **Thinkstock**: Photos.com 14br; **U.S. National Archives**: 27tr, 35cr.

Key: t = top, c = center, b = bottom, l = left, r = right.

Manufactured in the United States of America
1 2 3 4 5 6 7 8 9   12 11 10

CPSIA compliance information: Batch #CW13GS: For further information contact Gareth Stevens, New York, New York at 1-800-542-2595.

CONTENTS

INTRODUCTION

Before World War II began in Europe in 1939, Germany had been arming itself. It built tanks, submarines, and dive bombers, all of which had developed rapidly since World War I (1914–1918). At the start of World War II, Germany's tanks and Stuka dive bombers helped it conquer much of northern Europe. Its submarines—U-boats—threatened to starve Britain out of the war by destroying its merchant fleet.

The USS *Angler* was one of the Gato class of submarines. More than 300 vessels were built to the same template. It was the largest building program ever undertaken by the U.S. Navy.

Dive bomber: A small bomber that approaches its target in a vertical dive.

"Tika IV" was a P-41 Mustang. The U.S. fighter was useful for long-range missions. Tanks beneath the wings carried extra fuel.

THE ALLIED RESPONSE

The Allies—Britain, France, the United States, and the Soviet Union—developed their own weapons. Many were built in the United States by women who replaced male workers in factories. In the Soviet Union, whole factories were moved east, away from the fighting, so they could keep making tanks, airplanes, and guns.

The Allies built long-range bombers that could strike at targets in Europe and the Pacific. They built fighter planes to protect them. In the Pacific, they built submarines to sink Japanese merchant ships, and they built aircraft carriers. These "floating islands" were key to victory. They brought the air war to Japan's home islands.

Merchant ship: An unarmed cargo vessel used for trade.

25-POUNDER

The Ordnance QF (quick firing) 25-pounder was the standard field cannon of the British Army and Commonwealth forces. It got its name from the weight of its ammunition. It was used from 1940 onward and was constantly being improved. The 25-pounder had a circular firing platform so the gun could turn in any direction. It could also be aimed into the air, so it could also be used as a howitzer.

A member of a British gun crew prepares to load a shell into a 25-pounder. Used shell cases lie on the ground behind the gun.

Howitzer: An artillery gun that fires shells in a high arc, to pass over enemy defenses.

More than 12,000 25-pound-ers were produced during the war. The gun was used everywhere that British or Commonwealth forces fought.

A POPULAR GUN

The 25-pounder was popular with gunners because it was very reliable and didn't break down easily. It was suitable for all types of environment, including the deserts of North Africa.

The 25-pounder was highly mobile. Early models were towed by trucks or tractors, but later models were self-propelled. The gun had a high rate of fire. When its six-man crew worked hard, it could fire six to eight rounds per minute. The gun's maximum range was 13,400 yards (12,253 m).

EYEWITNESS

"It has been said with some authority that the 25-pounder, which was the main weapon of Canadian field artillery, was the first piece of artillery to be developed logically from 'the target backwards.'"

Guy G. Simonds
Commander, Canadian Army, World War II

Self-propelled: A gun that has an engine and wheels or tracks, so it can move on its own.

AIRCRAFT CARRIER

The USS *Enterprise* carried 90 aircraft. It had two hydraulic catapults to shoot the planes off the deck at a high enough speed for take-off.

B y World War II, aircraft carriers had taken the place of battleships as the most important type of warship. The "flat tops" formed floating airfields. The ships carried fighters and torpedo bombers designed to sink enemy vessels. The sea war in the Pacific was won by U.S. carriers and their pilots.

Hydraulic: Machinery powered by energy created by putting liquids under pressure.

TURNING POINT

When the Japanese attacked Pearl Harbor in Hawaii in December 1941, none of the eight U.S. carriers were at the base. By the end of the war, more than 30 carriers led the U.S. challenge to Japanese control of the Pacific.

The turning point of the Pacific War came at the Battle of Midway in June 1942. The Japanese thought the U.S. carriers had been sunk a month earlier. They were wrong. At Midway, 37 U.S. carrier bombers destroyed two Japanese carriers. Soon after, two more Japanese carriers were destroyed. The carriers had brought U.S. domination in the Pacific.

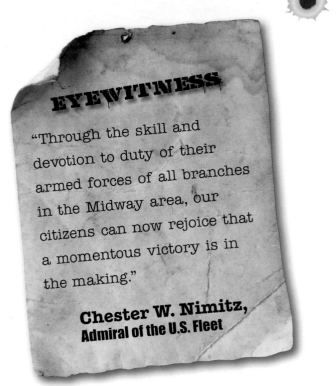

EYEWITNESS

"Through the skill and devotion to duty of their armed forces of all branches in the Midway area, our citizens can now rejoice that a momentous victory is in the making."

Chester W. Nimitz,
Admiral of the U.S. Fleet

A fighter plane flies above the USS *Enterprise*. Ropes across the deck caught hooks beneath the aircraft to stop the planes as they landed.

Pearl Harbor: The base of the U.S. Pacific Fleet in Hawaii, attacked by Japan on December 7, 1941.

B-17 FLYING FORTRESS

The B-17 was the bomber that brought the war to Germany. Flying at high altitude to avoid antiaircraft fire, B-17s flew frequent raids from August 1942. The B-17G was the most popular model: 8,680 were built. It was armed with 13 Browning machine guns and a remote-controlled turret under its nose.

The Flying Fortress had a crew of 10 men. The pilot and copilot were joined by an engineer, a navigator, a bombardier, a radio operator, and four gunners.

Bombardier: The member of a bomber crew whose job is to aim and drop the aircraft's bombs.

EYEWITNESS

"In my opinion the B-17 was the finest combat airplane the Air Force has ever had. It was capable of carrying much more weight than we ever put into it: the problem was the configuration of the bomb bay."

Lt. John Minahan
U.S. 19th Bomb Group,
Mareeba, Australia, 1942

B-17s fly in formation toward Germany on one of the "1,000-bomber" raids on German cities.

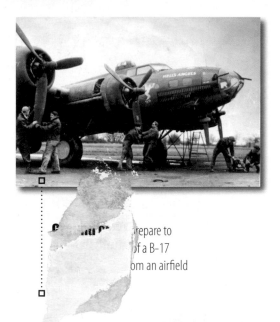

prepare to
of a B-17
om an airfield

FIGHTER PROTECTION

The Flying Fortress was extremely popular with pilots. It was reliable and easy to maneuver, and could survive heavy fire. Its range varied from 3,770 miles (6,034 km) unloaded to 1,110 miles (1,760 km) fully loaded with bombs.

Even with their strong armor and heavy firepower, the slow bombers risked being shot down. After 60 out of 291 planes were shot down during raids over southern Germany on October 14, 1943, unaccompanied bombing missions were halted. For protection, the bombers flew in tight formation with a fighter escort.

Ground crew: The mechanics who maintain an airplane and prepare it for flights.

Ground crew in the Marianas Islands prepare a Superfortress for a mission over Japan. The aircraft could carry 20,000 pounds (9,075 kg) of bombs.

B-29 SUPERFORTRESS

In 1940, it looked as though Britain might fall to the Nazis. The U.S. Air Force needed a long-range bomber that could reach Europe, if necessary. The answer was the B-29 Superfortress. The bomber deserved its "super" nickname. Its range was 3,250 miles (5,200 km). It was huge. Its maximum take-off weight was twice that of the B-17. And the B-29 was advanced. It was the first airplane to have a pressurized cabin as standard.

EYEWITNESS

"If Dante had been with us on the plane, he would have been terrified."

Paul Tibbets
Commander, *Enola Gay*, on bombing of Hiroshima

Dante: A 13th-century Italian poet who wrote about a vision of hell, called *Inferno*.

BOMBING JAPAN

In the end, Britain did not fall. But the B-29's long range made it vital in the Pacific. In summer 1944, the capture of Saipan in the Marianas brought the Japanese home islands within range. B-29s flew night-time raids to carpet bomb Japan. Wooden cities such as Tokyo burned in huge firestorms. Many thousands of people were killed.

The most famous B-29 was *Enola Gay*. On August 6, 1945, it dropped the first atomic bomb, "Little Boy," on the city of Hiroshima. Three days later, another B-29, *Bockscar*, dropped "Fat Man" on Nagasaki. The Japanese surrendered a few weeks later.

A formation of Superfortresses flies past Mount Fuji, a volcano in the middle of Japan and an important symbol of their homeland for the Japanese.

Carpet bomb: To saturate an area with bombs, rather than picking out individual targets.

BREN GUN

British gunners in Tobruk use a Bren gun to fire at Axis aircraft. British and Commonwealth troops were besieged in the Libyan port for 240 days in 1941.

The Bren was a light machine gun used by both the British and Canadian armies from 1938 onward. It was popular with infantrymen because it was easy to use and accurate. Based on a Czech weapon, the Bren gun used the same .303 ammunition as the standard British rifle, the Lee-Enfield. The Bren gun was fitted with a 30-round magazine. That meant the gun had to be reloaded frequently. This was sometimes helpful, as it stopped the barrel from overheating.

The Bren gun was usually supported by a bipod or tripod. Its curved magazine held 30 rounds.

Magazine: A metal case loaded with a number of cartridges ready to be clipped into a machine gun.

A British infantryman fires a Bren gun in northern France in 1944. The Bren gun was named for the place it was designed, Brno in Czechoslovakia.

ACCURATE AT RANGE

The Bren gun had a two-man team; one man fired and the other reloaded. All infantry units were equipped with a Bren gun, and all of the men in the unit shared the task of carrying the ammunition—and the Bren needed a lot of ammo. The gun was useful because of its long range. It was accurate up to 600 yards (550 m), with a maximum range of 1,850 yards (1,700 m). Later models were supported on a bipod or a tripod. This helped them become even more accurate, as they were more stable.

GUN CARRIER

The Bren gun carrier was a lightly armored tracked vehicle used to carry infantry into battle even under enemy fire. It was the most widely used armored fighting vehicle—AFV—among the Allied Forces. The three-man crew fired the Bren gun mounted in front of the vehicle as they traveled.

Armored fighting vehicle: A military vehicle protected by armor and equipped with weapons.

15

C-47 SKYTRAIN

The C-47 Skytrain, or Dakota, was not a warplane. But according to General Eisenhower, the supreme Allied commander, it was vital in winning the war. The transport plane allowed the U.S. military to move men and supplies quickly to where they were needed. It was adapted from a passenger jet, the Douglas DC-3.

A key role of the Skytrain was to fly over the Himalayas from India to China. The planes took supplies to Chinese nationalists and U.S. Air Force bases. Pilots called the mountain range "the Hump."

Transport plane: An aircraft that is adapted to carry large amounts of cargo or soldiers.

FLEXIBLE WORKHORSE

The Skytrain could carry 6,000 pounds (13,200 kg) of cargo, including a jeep, or a 37mm cannon, or 28 men in combat gear. It was used to drop paratroopers and for reconnaissance. For medical airlift, it had room for 14 stretcher patients and three nurses. With its reinforced floor, larger freight doors, and a more powerful engine than the civilian plane, the C-47 was a workhorse. It had a range of 3,800 miles (6,080 km).

A mechanic services a C-47 engine. The two engines were more powerful than the civilian model of the airplane.

Soldiers climb into a C-47 Dakota for a practice jump. The Dakota nickname came from Douglas Aircraft Company Transport Aircraft: DACoTA.

Reconnaissance: Gathering information by surveying enemy positions and strength.

HURRICANE

Although the Hawker Hurricane lived in the shadow of the Spitfire, it changed the future of fighter planes. In the Battle of Britain in 1940, the RAF had 32 squadrons of Hurricanes and only 19 of Spitfires. In the battle, Hurricanes shot down more than 80 percent of the planes lost by the Germans.

TWO Hurricanes fly in formation. When it entered service in 1937, the Hurricane became the RAF's first monoplane fighter.

Monoplane: An aircraft with only one wing on either side.

There were special versions of the Hurricane for use in the desert, in tropical conditions, or at sea.

Pilots run to get their Hurricanes airborne during the Battle of Britain in 1940.

CANVAS BODY

The Hurricane was super strong. The framework of its body was made from steel tubing. It was covered in canvas. That meant that it could withstand damage that would destroy most fighters. With eight machine guns on its wings, it could fire 150 bullets per second.

As the war went on, the Hurricane was used less as a fighter and more as a bomber. The Mark II was an improved fighter–bomber. In the Mediterranean and North Africa, it was used to attack vehicles on the ground with rockets, bombs, and added guns.

EYEWITNESS

"It was a delightful aeroplane—not as agile as a Spitfire, but it had a very good gun platform. It was very steady and took a tremendous amount of battle damage without appearing to worry too much."

RGA Barclay
Pilot officer, RAF

Battle of Britain: The air battle between the RAF and the Luftwaffe over England in 1940.

KATYUSHA

Named for a popular song, the Katyusha, or "little Katy," was a Soviet rocket launcher. It could fire multiple rockets at the same time, but it wasn't very accurate and took a long time to reload. However, it was cheap, and it could be easily mounted on top of different vehicles like tanks or trucks.

One advantage of the Katyusha was that it was light and easy to move. Trucks could be positioned to deliver a devastating barrage on a target.

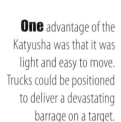

Barrage: A large amount of shells or bombs delivered on one place at the same time.

MULTIPLE LAUNCHER

The Katyusha could carry up to 48 launching pipes. There were several versions. The most common was the BM-13. It had a range of 5.29 miles (8.47 km). Its rockets weighed 93 pounds (42 kg) and were nearly 6 feet (180 cm) long.

A distinguishing feature of the Katyusha was a distinctive whine it made when a rocket was launched. The sound demoralized the Germans. It sounded a little like a church organ, so the Germans nicknamed the weapon "Stalin's Organ."

NAMED FOR A GIRL

The Katyusha's unusual nickname came from a popular Soviet wartime song, "Katyusha." The song is about a girl who is missing her boyfriend, who is away fighting in the war. The association may have begun because the rockets were all stamped with the letter K, for the factory where they were made.

Rockets streak into the night sky from a whole row of Katyushas mounted on top of tracked tractors.

Rocket: A missile that is powered by its own fuel and propulsion unit.

LANCASTER BOMBER

Ten versions of the Lancaster were produced, but none of them was very different from the original 1942 model.

The British four-engined Avro Lancaster was a heavy bomber used in Europe from early 1942. It was the main aircraft used in the RAF's campaign of night raids on German cities. Its 33-foot (10-m) long bomb bay allowed it to carry huge bombs. Tallboys were 5-ton (5,445-kg) "earthquake bombs" that could destroy even strengthened defensive positions. They also sank the famous German battleship, *Tirpitz*, in November 1944.

Battleship: The most heavily armed type of warship.

THE BOMBER

The most famous Lancaster mission was the Dambuster raid of 1943. The targets were dams in Germany's Ruhr Valley. The Lancasters of 617 Squadron carried special "bouncing bombs." The bombs skipped along the surface of the lakes behind the dams, then sank and blew up next to the dam wall. To get the bombs to bounce, the pilots had to fly just 60 feet (18 m) above the water, at 240 miles per hour (390 km/h).

EYEWITNESS

"I felt a little remote and unreal sitting up there in the warm cockpit of my Lancaster, watching this mighty power which we had unleashed…"

Guy Gibson
Squadron commander,
Dambuster raid

A Lancaster is fueled and loaded with bombs. The bomber had a crew of seven men, including pilots, bombers, and gunners.

Cockpit: The part of an airplane where the pilot and copilot sit.

LIBERTY SHIP

By 1940 the German plan to starve Britain into surrender by sinking cargo ships in the Atlantic Ocean was paying off. The British needed to replace lost ships. Using an adopted British idea, U.S. shipyards began one of the biggest industrial programs ever. They set out to replace and increase the numbers of cargo ships in the Atlantic. Between 1941 and 1945, 18 U.S. shipyards built a remarkable 2,710 ships.

The *Jeremiah O'Brien* is one of the few surviving Liberty ships. All the ships were built to the same template, so they all looked identical.

Template: A plan that gives the shapes and dimensions of pieces used in construction.

A woman worker checks the welded seam between sections of a Liberty ship.

The USS *Robert E. Peary* was built as a publicity stunt in just 4.5 days. It was constructed in the shipyards of Henry Kaiser, who oversaw the Liberty ship program.

RECORDBREAKERS

At the start of the war, it took about 230 days to build a merchant ship. The so-called Liberty ships could be built in just 42 days. One ship was built in just 4 days and 15.5 hours as a publicity stunt. Many of the workers were women who did the jobs formerly done by men who were now away fighting. The ships were all built to the same plan. They were made of stainless steel sections welded together. Welding speeded things up; it was quicker than riveting the metal together.

FDR'S NAME

The Liberty ships got their name from U.S. president Franklin D. Roosevelt. He recalled a Founding Father of the United States, Patrick Henry, who said, "Give me liberty or give me death!" Launching the ship-building program in September 1941, Roosevelt said, "There must be liberty, worldwide and eternal." The ships were part of achieving that aim.

Riveting: A method of joining pieces of metal together with flat-headed bolts.

M-2 FLAMETHROWER

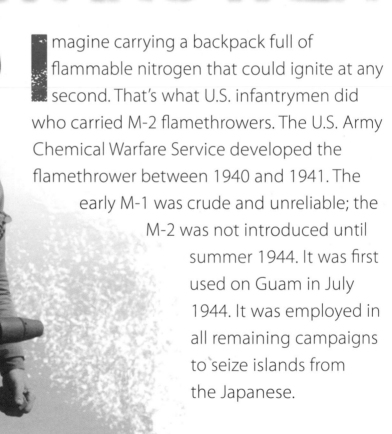

Imagine carrying a backpack full of flammable nitrogen that could ignite at any second. That's what U.S. infantrymen did who carried M-2 flamethrowers. The U.S. Army Chemical Warfare Service developed the flamethrower between 1940 and 1941. The early M-1 was crude and unreliable; the M-2 was not introduced until summer 1944. It was first used on Guam in July 1944. It was employed in all remaining campaigns to seize islands from the Japanese.

This U.S. infantryman is carrying an M-2 on a Pacific island. The weapon was useful against enemies who hid in thick vegetation.

Flammable: Something that catches fire and burns easily.

FLAMETHROWER

Unlike the M-1, the M-2 did not rely on electrical ignition. Instead, it used special cartridges to light the gas. The cartridges were stored in a drum at the tip of the flame tube.

U.S. Marine units used a tactic called "corkscrew and blowtorch." They used heavy machine fire to allow flamethrowers to get close to their targets. The weapon could fire flames in bursts of about 7 seconds. At a range of 20 to 40 yards (18–36 m), the flames would destroy everything. Later flamethrowers were increasingly replaced by flamethrowing tanks.

A U.S. soldier uses an M-2 to set fire to a building that might shelter Japanese troops during fighting for Namur, one of the Marshall Islands.

Ignition: The act of starting a machine by setting fire to its fuel.

29

M1 GARAND RIFLE

The rifle nicknamed the "GI's best friend" was the first semiautomatic to become standard issue for the U.S. military in 1936. It was accurate at long range, and fired rapidly with little recoil. The rifle was popular with soldiers because it was highly reliable and rarely jammed. That more than made up for the fact that it was a little heavy.

A U.S. paratrooper carries his M1 as his patrol uses a churchyard wall for shelter while searching a French village in June 1944.

The M1 was a standard weapon. More than 5.5 million were produced.

Recoil: The thrust that pushes a gun backward when it fires.

SEMIAUTOMATIC RIFLE

The M1 was a semiautomatic. That meant that the gas given off by firing a round pushed the next round into the chamber from a clip of eight or ten powerful .30 Springfield shells. The gun fired a round every time the trigger was pulled, up to 30 rounds per minute. That gave U.S. soldiers a clear advantage over the bolt-action rifles with which their enemies were usually armed. The Garand had a range of about 440 yards (400 m). More than 6.25 million M1 rifles were manufactured before they were taken out of service in the early 1960s.

U.S. soldiers load their M1s during a firefight with Germans in northern France.

P-47 THUNDERBOLT

American pilots named the Republic Aviation P-47 "the Jug." British pilots said the nickname was short for "juggernaut." The Thunderbolt was the heaviest single-engine fighter. The plane weighed up to 8 tons (7.9 t). Pilots complained that it was like flying a bath tub. But the P-47 could carry a bombload that was nearly half that of the B-17 Flying Fortress, a dedicated bomber.

A P-47 Thunderbolt (front) escorts an F-17 Flying Fortress. Escort duty was one of the main tasks for the P-47.

Juggernaut: A slang word for a massive, slow-moving truck.

Ground crew prepare belts of 0.50in shells to load into a Thunderbolt's eight machine guns.

The P-47's propeller was a giant 12 feet (3.65 m) across.

TWO ROLES

The Thunderbolt had two main roles. It was an effective escort plane that could take on enemy fighters in high-altitude dogfights. It was also an outstanding ground-attack aircraft. As a fighter-bomber it could carry up to 2,500 pounds (1,135 kg) of bombs or rockets. Its eight 0.5 caliber machine guns could strafe targets on the ground. The whole aircraft was solid enough to withstand damage. The cockpit was armored, so that the pilot had additional protection.

DIVE BOMBER

The Germans' most effective ground-attack aircraft was the JU-87 Stuka. In the lightning attacks of the Blitzkrieg at the start of the war, the plane would dive almost vertically to release its bombs. A siren on its leg gave out a wail that terrified people on the ground. A bent "gull wing" made the airplane better at diving and easier to maneuver. The acceleration of diving could make the pilot black out. The airplane had special air brakes that would bring it out of its dive if that happened.

The first Mustang was an average machine. The addition of a Rolls Royce engine turned it into probably the best fighter of the war.

P-51 MUSTANG

The American P-51 Mustang, with its British Rolls Royce Merlin engine, was perhaps the best fighter of World War II. It was certainly the most important fighter in terms of numbers. Nearly 15,000 Mustangs were built. They destroyed 4,950 enemy aircraft in Europe, giving them the highest strike rate of any U.S. fighter.

EYEWITNESS

"The thing that really set the Mustang apart from any other fighter, friend or foe, was its range. With a 75-gallon tank slung under each wing, it could perform the unheard-of: It could fly six-hour missions."

**Capt. Robert Goebel
31st Fighter group,
Twelfth Airforce**

Strike rate: The av___ ___mbe_ ___ _own per fighter.

LONGER RANGE

The Mustang's great advantage over other fighters was its range. It could fly 908 miles (1,500 km), which took it deep into enemy territory. The Mustang escorted U.S. bombers on raids on Germany's industrial heartland. The fighter was armed with six 12.7mm Browning machine guns fixed in its wings. It could be used as a dive bomber, bomber escort, ground-attacker, or interceptor. It was far superior to anything the Germans possessed. Hermann Goering was the head of the Luftwaffe, the German air force. He said that when he saw Mustangs over Berlin, he knew Germany had lost the war.

Andrew D. Turner was one of the Tuskegee Airmen, the only African-American pilots who flew in the U.S. Army Corps while the military services were still segregated.

Underwing fuel tanks meant that Mustangs based in Britain could escort bombers all the way to the German capital, Berlin, and back.

PPSH-41 SUBMACHINE GUN

The PPSh-41 was a Soviet submachine gun produced in huge numbers for the Red Army from 1941. It was designed for conscripts with little training. They needed a gun that was easy to fire and reliable, but which didn't need much looking after. The gun had to be suitable for close-quarter forest and urban fighting.

The round magazine of the PPSh-41 could hold 35 rounds of ammunition. Holes in the sides of the barrel helped keep the gun cool.

Conscripts: Untrained civilians who are forced to serve in the army.

The PPSh-41 was easy to make. More than 5 million were produced in just three years.

MASS PRODUCTION

The gun had to be cheap and quick to produce. It used a new technology called metal pressing, so only the barrel and the drum magazine were expensive. Between 1941 and 1945, five million of the weapons were produced.

Like other Soviet weapons, the PPSh had to withstand freezing temperatures. It could fire 900 rounds per minute. Although it was heavy to carry, it could fire 5,000 rounds before it needed to be cleaned.

This Russian partisan carries a PPSh-41. The weapon was ideal for partisans because it was easy to maintain.

ENEMY WEAPONS

The German Army recognized the great qualities of the PPSh. They captured so many during their invasion of the Soviet Union that they were able to use them against their enemies, including Soviet forces. The Germans began a program to convert the captured guns into the standard German submachine gun, the 9mm Parabellum.

Partisan: Someone who fights in an armed resistance group in occupied territory.

SHERMAN TANK

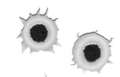

The U.S. Sherman was a key Allied medium tank. The Sherman M4 appeared at El Alamein in North Africa in 1942. After that, it appeared wherever the Allies fought. It was produced in huge numbers. On the Western Front, some 30,000 Shermans faced 2,000 German Tiger tanks.

The Sherman M4 was the most widely produced of all Allied tanks. More than 40,000 were built after it first appeared at El Alamein in October 1942.

Medium tank: A tank that is quite heavily armored, but still light enough to move quickly.

A Sherman rumbles ashore from a Landing Ship, Tank (LST) in Normandy in the aftermath of D-Day, June 1944.

A Sherman commander looks out over a valley during the Allies advance in southern Italy in 1943.

OVER THE EDGE

Later versions of the tank were well armed with a 17-pounder (7.62-kg) gun that could take on Germany's heavy tanks at long range. Its powered turret allowed the crew to turn the gun and fire more quickly than the enemy.

The Sherman had three advantages over German tanks. It was reliable and easy to fix. It was very strong. And it could be mass-produced quickly and cheaply. But it had a weaker engine and gun, although the gun was later improved. Its narrow tracks meant that it could sink in soft ground. And the Sherman had a reputation for catching fire easily. The troops called it the "Ronson," for a type of lighter.

Turret: The top part of a tank, which carries the main gun and can revolve.

SPITFIRE

The Supermarine Spitfire is the most famous of all British fighter planes. It played a key part in the Allied victory in the Battle of Britain in the summer and fall of 1940. It was quicker than other fighters and was easy to maneuver. That meant it could dodge gunfire in "dogfights" with enemy fighters. Its cannon and Browning machine guns gave it serious firepower. The airplane was the main fighter of the Royal Air Force in World War II.

Spitfires fly above southern England in the summer of 1940. The Spitfire was a match for German fighters because of its great maneuverability.

Dogfight: A one-on-one battle in which two fighter planes try to shoot each other down.

"When I was first given one to fly, my first emotion was almost intimidation. [The fighter] felt like a thoroughbred horse watching a new rider coming up. But once I was inside, the Spitfire, quite frankly, flew me."

Geoffrey Wellum
Squadron leader, RAF

BATTLE OF BRITAIN

The Spitfire made its maiden flight on March 5, 1940. It was the latest in aircraft technology. British air chiefs were so impressed they ordered 370 to be built. Supermarine got them all ready in time to fight in the Battle of Britain later in the year.

The Spitfire was designed as a short-range fighter plane. It could carry two 250-pound (113-kg) bombs. It was also useful for photo reconnaissance, which was used extensively to locate enemy positions and to survey damage caused by bombing raids.

A surviving Spitfire takes to the air. There were five different models of the plane, which was originally designed by R. J. Mitchell.

Maiden flight: Another term for a debut, or first, flight.

SUBMARINE

The Germans had used *Unterseeboots*—U-boats—in World War I to sink Allied ships. U-boat "wolf packs" also hunted merchant convoys in the Atlantic early in World War II. But German success in the Atlantic was outstripped by the success of U.S. submarines in the Pacific. Submarines made up less than 2 percent of the vessels of the U.S. Navy, but they sank more than 30 percent of Japan's surface fleet.

The USS *Nautilus* had a long range, so it was used as a tanker to take air fuel to island airbases. It was also used to get raiding forces ashore on occupied islands.

Occupied: Land that is in the control of the enemy.

UNDER WATER

When the United States entered the war after the attack on Pearl Harbor on December 7, 1941, there were only 14 working U.S. subs in the Pacific. Another 130 were built during the war. The Japanese relied on imports of oil, food, and other supplies. The U.S. campaign strangled the economy by sinking over five million tons of merchant shipping. The largest single victim was the aircraft carrier *Shinano*.

A U.S. submarine captain uses a periscope to study the movement of ships on the surface of the ocean above.

The submarines fired torpedoes to damage ships beneath the waterline. Conditions were so cramped the crew slept among the torpedoes.

U-BOATS

German U-boats were the Nazis' most effective weapon in the Battle of the Atlantic. Germany's submarine fleet sank almost 3,000 Allied merchant ships. Its aim was to starve Britain into submission. As the war went on, the Allies got better at defending convoys against sub attack.

Periscope: A tube fitted with mirrors that allows people in submarines to see the ocean surface.

T-34 TANK

The T-34 had relatively large wheels. That made it quite quick and also helped it to cross wide obstacles, such as ditches.

The T-34 was the tank that beat the Wehrmacht. This Soviet tank had a high velocity gun and an electrically operated turret. Its turret armor was over 2 inches (52 mm) thick. Its tracks were easy to maintain and were kept in place by simple plates on the body of the tank. More that 40,000 T-34s were built. In July 1943, the T-34 took on German Panzers at the Battle of Kursk, the largest tank battle in history.

Panzer: The German name for a tank.

A MATCH FOR THE PANZERS

The T-34's sloping armor made it difficult for German shells to score a direct hit. Meanwhile its own 3-inch (76.2-mm) gun could destroy a German Panzer before it was within the Panzer's range. The T-34 used less flammable fuel than the U.S. Sherman tank, so it was less likely to catch fire if hit. Its wide tracks let it cross any kind of terrain and didn't get stuck in mud. The Germans were so impressed by the T-34 that they copied some of its features into the Panther tanks they began to produce in mid-1943 to take on the T-34s.

A four-man crew pose with their T-34. The tank had a commander, a driver, a loader, and a gunner (in some models, the commander also had to fire the main gun).

PANZER TANKS

The German tactic of Blitzkrieg—"lightning war"—relied on tanks. The Panzers broke through defenses and made rapid advances, backed up by aircraft, artillery, and infantry. The Panzers had stormed through Poland, France, Belgium, and the Netherlands. Before they met the T-34 in 1941, the Panzers had been the supreme battlefield tank of the war. Now they had to be upgraded, eventually becoming the Panzer V, or the Panther.

Terrain: The physical shape and characteristics of an area of ground.

GLOSSARY

amphibious: Something that can operate on land or in the water.

armored fighting vehicle: A military vehicle protected by armor and equipped with weapons.

barrage: A large amount of shells or bombs delivered at the same time.

Battle of Britain: The air battle between the RAF and the Luftwaffe over England in 1940.

battleship: The most heavily armed type of warship.

bombardier: The member of a bomber crew whose job is to aim and drop the aircraft's bombs.

carpet bomb: To saturate an area with bombs, rather than picking out individual targets.

cockpit: The part of an airplane where the pilot and copilot sit.

conscripts: Untrained civilians who are forced to serve in the army.

firefight: A close-range gunfight in which both sides fire at the other.

gatling gun: A machine gun with multiple rotating barrels.

ground crew: The mechanics who maintain an airplane and prepare it for flights.

Luftwaffe: The official name of Germany's air force.

magazine: A metal case loaded with a number of cartridges ready to be clipped into a machine gun.

partisan: Someone who fights in a resistance group in occupied territory.

Pearl Harbor: The base of the U.S. Pacific Fleet in Hawaii, attacked by Japan on December 7, 1941.

recoil: The thrust that pushes a gun backward when it fires.

reconnaissance: Gathering information by surveying enemy positions.

rocket: A missile that is powered by its own fuel and propulsion unit.

strafe: To fire from the air at targets on the ground.

transport plane: An aircraft that is adapted to carry large amounts of cargo or soldiers.

FURTHER INFORMATION

BOOKS

Burgan, Michael. *Weapons, Gear, and Uniforms of World War II* (Edge Books). Capstone Press, 2012.

Doeden, Matt. *Weapons of World War II* (Blazers: Weapons of War). Capstone Press, 2008.

Graham, Ian. *You Wouldn't Want to Be a World War II Pilot*. Turtleback, 2009.

Hamilton, John. *Weapons* (World War II). Abdo Publishing Co., 2011.

Orr, Tamra. *The Atom Bomb: Creating and Exploring the First Nuclear Weapon*. Rosen Publishing Group, 2004.

Stein, R. Conrad. *World War II in the Pacific: From Pearl Harbor to Nagasaki* (The United States at War). Enslow Publishing Inc, 2011.

WEBSITES

http://www.historylearningsite.co.uk/ weapons_of_world_war_two.htm
History Learning Site page with links to facts about major weapons.

http://www.toptenz.net/top-10-wwii-infantry-weapons.php
Top 10 infantry weapons of the war.

http://military.discovery.com/history/ world-war-2/world-war-2.html
The Military Channel guide to weapons and technology in World War II.

http://history.howstuffworks.com/ world-war-ii/historical-introduction-to-world-war-ii5.htm
HowStuffWorks page on weapons and tactics of World War II.

INDEX